Nature's Children

MOUNTAIN GOATS

Bill Ivy

GROLIER
EDUCATIONAL

FACTS IN BRIEF

Classification of the Mountain Goat
    Class: *Mammalia* (mammals)
    Order: *Artiodactyla* (cloven-hoofed mammals)
    Family: *Bovidae* (antelopes, cattle, sheep, goats)
    Genus: *Oreamnos*
    Species: *Oreamnos americanus*

World distribution. Exclusive to the North American West.

Habitat. Mountain slopes, usually above the tree line.

Distinctive physical characteristics. White coat all year round, black hoofs, bearded, both male and female have short black horns.

Habits. Active during the day, females and young live in small herds, males usually live alone or in small groups.

Diet. Grasses, rushes, shrubs, trees.

Published originally as
"Getting to Know . . . Nature's Children."

This series is approved and recommended
by the Federation of Ontario Naturalists.

This library reinforced edition is available exclusively from:

GROLIER
EDUCATIONAL

Sherman Turnpike, Danbury, Connecticut 06816

Contents

Have you ever wished you could climb a high mountain? The icy winds and jagged cliffs are a challenge only a few people are brave enough to meet. It takes a lot of training, skill and equipment to scale the peak. Even with all that, however, the most expert mountaineer is no match for the incredible Mountain Goat. This nimble-footed animal moves with ease through remote mountain terrain where one slip up could send it tumbling to its death.

Until recently, very little was known about the Mountain Goat since it inhabits such remote areas. Read along and discover what we now know about these adventurous creatures.

Kidding Around

Like all children, young Mountain Goats, or kids, love to play. They are very frisky and will spend hours chasing each other, scrambling up rocks and jumping off, or racing up to the edge of a steep bank and stopping just in time to avoid falling over. Now and then, they pause to nibble on a few blades of grass or a tasty mountain bluebell. When at last they have tired themselves out, they drift back to snuggle down and rest beside their mothers, who have been keeping a close watch over them.

Life is not all fun and games, however. There are lessons to be learned. By following their mothers up craggy cliffs and along dangerous ledges, the kids soon become skilled little mountaineers.

I'm the king of the castle!

Head in the Clouds

Mountain Goats are found in the mountainous regions of western North America, as far north as Alaska and south to the states of Oregon and Idaho. They make their home in some of the world's most rugged terrain and generally settle close to the timberline, often as high as 2500 metres (8 000 feet) above sea level. During the winter they move to slightly lower elevations. Mountain Goats do not usually have much company, since few other animals can survive in this snowy land among the clouds!

The shaded area on this map shows where Mountain Goats live.

Kinfolk

When is a goat not a goat? When it is a Mountain Goat!

Despite its name, the Mountain Goat is not really a goat at all but is actually more closely related to the antelope family. Its closest relatives are a small group of mountain antelopes—the serow and goral of Asia and the chamois of the European Alps.

Many people confuse the Mountain Goat with the Dall's Sheep, the only other large, white mammal found in the mountains. From a distance they may look similar, but they are not related and they inhabit different areas. There is no other animal quite like the Mountain Goat in North America.

Even Mountain Goats enjoy a nice bath—a dust bath that is!

Woolly Wardrobe

The Mountain Goat is well dressed for its life in the mountains. It wears a heavy, white fleecy coat which keeps it snug and warm regardless of the weather. The shaggy outer layer is made up of guard hairs that may be up to 15 centimetres (6 inches) long and that shed both water and snow. Underneath are as much as 9 centimetres (3 to 4 inches) of very fine wool. This lovely soft undercoat helps to keep the Mountain Goat's valuable body heat from escaping.

The Indians of North America's northwest coast once used the woolly undercoat of the Mountain Goat for making their beautiful Chilkat blankets. These blankets were well known for being both lightweight and warm.

No matter how cold the wind, it cannot penetrate these warm woollies.

Hill Billies and Nannies

While the Mountain Goat may not be a goat, it certainly looks like one. It is much more stocky and heavy, however, than the familiar domestic goat. The males, known as billies, can weigh 113 kilograms (250 pounds) or more and may stand over 110 centimetres (43 inches) at the shoulder. Females, or nannies, are much lighter and shorter.

Both the nannies and the billies have beards and slender black horns. The billies' horns are gently curved while those of the nannies are straighter and curve sharply at the tips. Unlike the antlers of deer or moose, a Mountain Goat's horns will never fall off. They appear very soon after the Mountain Goat is born and continue to grow a little longer each year.

Mountain Goats walk very stiffly, and this gives them an air of dignity. In truth, their noble strut is due to their short front legs rather than their position in life.

One look at this goat's horns tells you that she's a nanny.

Amazing Feet

When it comes to climbing, the Mountain Goat is in a class of its own. It travels with complete confidence along ledges so narrow that it seems to be walking on air. Even rock faces that seem to us to go straight up are climbed with ease. How does the Mountain Goat accomplish these astonishing feats?

For one thing it has a very cool head and obviously it is not afraid of heights. It also has an amazing sense of balance. But, the real secret lies in the design of its feet. The Mountain Goat's hoofs have a hard outer edge for cutting into rock or ice. The center is filled with a soft rubber pad that gives traction. In addition the sole of each foot is slightly hollowed and acts something like a suction cup when pressed down.

Unlike a horse's hoof, which is all in one piece, the Mountain Goat's hoof is split into two "toes." These can be spread wide to prevent the animal from slipping when traveling downhill. Two claws higher up the foot serve as brakes should the goat begin to slide.

The underside of a Mountain Goat's hoof.

Amazing Feats

Years ago it was believed that if a Mountain Goat fell off a cliff it would land on its horns and bounce back up unharmed. Although this is certainly a tall tale, the Mountain Goat is in fact capable of feats that would make a circus performer envious!

Should one of these agile mountaineers run out of room on a ledge, it can either back up or rise up on its hind legs, turn right around and drop down safely on all fours. Moreover, it can jump from one bit of ledge to another, covering as much as 3 metres (10 feet) in a single bound.

And if a Mountain Goat wants to move to a higher ledge, it can leap straight up and hook its front feet over the top of the rock—much as you might do with your arms. With help from its back legs, it then pulls itself up over the ridge to the top. Not bad for a heavyweight!

Even the best of us make mistakes, however, and Mountain Goats are no exception. Sadly, one will on occasion lose its footing and fall to its death.

Opposite page:
Only the surefooted travel here.

Super Senses

It is almost impossible to sneak up on a
Mountain Goat. Its dark round eyes are
blackbird sharp and can spot movement at least
1500 metres (1 mile) away! In order to get a
better view of its surroundings, the Mountain
Goat has the curious habit of sitting on its
haunches the way a dog does.

Strangely the Mountain Goat is not as aware
of motion when approached from above.
However, its keen sense of smell usually detects
an enemy long before there is any danger.
Should the scent be lost in shifting breezes, the
goat still has its sensitive ears to warn it. Believe
it or not, an experienced adult has such
well-developed hearing that it can tell the
difference between rocks falling naturally and
those dropping because of an approaching
intruder.

Who goes there?

Mountain Menaces

High in its alpine home, the Mountain Goat is usually safe from enemies. Few animals dare venture into such rough territory. While a golden eagle may swoop down from the sky and snatch away a very young Mountain Goat, only the cougar and the lynx are surefooted enough to be a threat on the ground. And even these predators are rarely able to get close enough to strike.

Should the Mountain Goat move into the valleys for food, however, it is in much more danger. In these areas, grizzly bears, coyotes, wolves and wolverines may also attack.

When threatened the Mountain Goat knows how to defend itself. Few animals are brave—or foolish—enough to take on its dagger-sharp horns, and those that have done so have ended up the worse for the encounter.

Of much greater danger to the goat are rock slides and avalanches. Several members of a herd can be buried should the snow on a mountainside give way. In fact, more Mountain Goats die this way than by any other means.

Opposite page:

No one is going to get my goat!

22

Slim Pickin's

In the harsh land of the Mountain Goat, food is often hard to find. Still Mountain Goats somehow manage to find enough plants to keep themselves alive. Grasses, sedges and rushes make up the bulk of their diet, but they also browse on trees and shrubs whenever they get the chance. Although they feed throughout the day, their main meals are breakfast and dinner.

Do you like the taste of salt? Well, Mountain Goats certainly do. They will travel great distances just to visit a natural salt lick. How about the taste of clay? That's right. Clay! Believe it or not, Mountain Goats like to snack on a special type of clay that is found high in the mountains. Using their sharp teeth, they nip off chunks of this earthy meal and chew it up as you would a carrot.

The Mountain Goat's strong, sharp teeth are ideal for snipping off tasty twigs.

Overleaf:
Enjoying a cool refreshing drink.

Leftovers Again!

What do deer, cows and Mountain Goats have in common? They all eat first and chew later.

Instead of chewing its food well before swallowing, the Mountain Goat gulps down its meal almost whole. The unchewed food is stored in a special part of the animal's stomach. Then when the goat feels like relaxing, it brings this food back up into its mouth and chews it at its leisure. This is known as "chewing the cud." Once the goat has done all the chewing it wants, the cud is once again swallowed for digestion in another part of the stomach.

Chewing the cud.

Mountain Bands

In Mountain Goat society, the nannies are the bosses (except during the mating season). Most billies live alone or in small loose groups during the summer, then join up with the females and their young. They soon learn their place as the high-ranking females keep them in line with their sharp horns.

The males, females and young Mountain Goats live together through the winter in bands of up to 20 members. While the herd is feeding, a sentinel stands guard, and keeps a close watch for any sign of danger.

The band does not usually travel very far. Its home range is often no more than 8 kilometres (5 miles). The goats spend a lot of time lying down in shallow depressions which they scoop out of the rock or ground.

Get Your Goat

Whenever they meet, billies usually get along fairly well—that is until the mating season, which occurs in late fall. Then they start bickering over whose nanny is whose.

Should two males want the same female, things may get rather tense. The angry billies stand head to tail daring each other to make a move. They arch their backs and stand tall, and if one of them does not give in, they might come to blows. Using their horns as daggers these white knights lunge sideways at each other. Usually the fighting does not last long, but it can become quite violent and result in serious injuries. Luckily, few battles actually take place.

The victorious males have a peculiar way of impressing the nannies. They crawl on their bellies and bleat like lambs. Don't laugh, it works!

A big billie.

Nanny's Nursery

In late spring, the nanny gives birth. For a nursery she selects a sheltered spot such as a cave or grassy ledge on a cliff. Usually one baby, or kid, is born but twins are not uncommon. On rare occasions triplets surprise their mother.

Immediately after the kid is born the nanny licks its wet, woolly coat dry. Unlike its mother, the newborn Mountain Goat may have prominent streaks of brown hair down its back. On top of its head are two black leathery spots where horns will soon grow.

Within minutes of its birth, the trembling kid struggles to its feet and soon begins to feed on its mother's milk. As it nurses it wags its stubby tail just like a barnyard goat. Only 33 centimetres (13 inches) tall at the shoulder and weighing about 3 kilograms (7 pounds), the newborn kid grows stronger every minute.

Keeping close to Mom.

New Kid on the Block

In less than an hour the wide-eyed kid is hopping around on its stilty legs. It follows its mother very closely, bleating softly whenever it wants to nurse. The nanny is careful to keep her baby hidden among the rocks whenever she wanders out to feed. She never stays away too long since the kid is totally dependent on her for food and protection.

At the first sign of danger the young goat will either drop to the ground and freeze or scramble beneath its mother. Any animal that might want to harm the kid must get by the nanny first! After a few days the mother and her kid come out of isolation and join the band of other nannies and their young.

When only one week old the kids begin to nibble on vegetation, but they will continue to drink their mother's milk for another five weeks or so. They grow quickly and by winter they weigh about 10 kilograms (22 pounds).

The young will stay with their mothers through the winter, but come spring, the nannies will send them off on their own before the new kids are born.

The rejected youngsters do not go very far, however. Most continue to ''hang around'' with the band for at least another year.

These kids' horns are already growing. By winter they will be about 9 centimetres (3-1/2 inches) long.

Hard Times

Winter in Mountain Goat country is extremely harsh. It is hard to believe that any creature could survive the freezing temperature and deep snowfalls. Yet the hardy Mountain Goats manage to endure the worst that this season has to offer. Staying warm is not really a problem as their extra-thick coats keep them cozy and dry. During particularly bad storms the goats may take shelter in a cave or beneath a rock ledge.

Mountain Goats often abandon the uppermost part of their range in the wintertime.

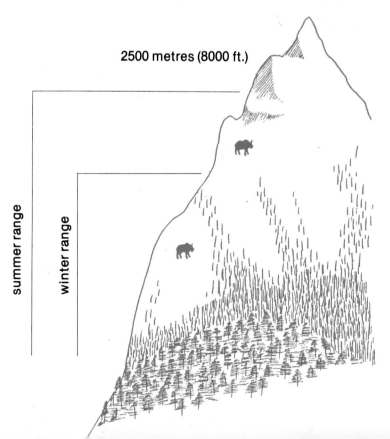

2500 metres (8000 ft.)

summer range

winter range

On the other hand, finding enough food to eat can be difficult in this winter wonderland. Should the snow become too deep to paw through, the goats will move to lower altitudes and settle on steeper, windblown slopes where the snow is not so deep and the plants are more exposed.

Even in these areas, food is never plentiful at this time of the year, and the Mountain Goats will not get much more than they need to keep alive. One result is that their horns grow more slowly, forming a narrower growth ring between those that form over the rest of the year. By counting these narrow rings as you would those of a tree trunk, you can tell the number of winters the goat has lived. The average Mountain Goat lives about ten rings.

Overleaf:

Explorer Captain James Cook reported seeing polar bears high on the cliffs when he visited North America. What he probably saw were these monarchs of the mountains.

Change of Clothes

When the first warm weather of spring arrives, it is time for the Mountain Goat to change out of its heavy winter coat into something a little more comfortable. Gradually, over the next couple of months, its fleece begins to thin out. Large patches of it are shed and catch on rocks and bushes.

At this stage, the Mountain Goat looks very scraggly, with many clumps of wool hanging from its body. However, before too long, a new lightweight summer coat grows in. This outfit gradually begins to thicken in the fall. New guard hairs grow and a thick undercoat develops just in time for the next long cold winter.

Caught changing!

Goat Watching

Unless you are willing to do a lot of climbing you will probably never see a Mountain Goat up close. A good pair of binoculars are a must for the serious goat watcher. Today, the majority of Mountain Goats are found in government parks. Even so, there are not that many of them living in the wild, so consider yourself lucky if you do happen to see one.

Who knows, perhaps you will one day be adventurous enough to visit these beautiful beasts in their natural environment and see first hand some of the things you have just read about.

Mountain Goat Track

The underside of a Mountain Goat's hoof.

Some Mountain Goats are as curious about us as we are about them.

Words to Know

Avalanche   A mass of snow, rock and ice that runs down a mountain quickly and suddenly.

Band   A group of Mountain Goats.

Billy   A male Mountain Goat.

Browse   Feed on.

Cud   Hastily swallowed food brought back for chewing by cud chewers such as deer, cows and Mountain Goats.

Guard hairs   Long coarse hairs that make up the outer layer of the Mountain Goat's coat.

Kid   A young Mountain Goat.

Mating season   The time of year during which animals come together to produce young.

Nanny   A female Mountain Goat.

Nurse   To drink the mother's milk.

Predator   An animal that hunts other animals for food.

Sedge   Grass-like plant.

Sentinel   A guard that watches for danger and signals alarm if necessary.

Timberline   The point of elevation in mountainous regions beyond which no trees grow.

INDEX

Cover Photo: T.W. Hall, Environment Canada.
Photo Credits: Brian Milne (First Light), pages 4, 14, 20, 24, 46; Thomas Kitchen, pages 8, 13, 17, 37, 44; Thomas Kitchen (Valan), page 7; Esther Schmidt (Valan), pages 11, 23; Pat Morrow (First Light), page 18; Dennis A. Schmidt (Valan), pages 26-27, 31, 34; Albert Kuhnick (First Light), pages 28, 40; Halle Flygare (Valan), page 33; Robert C. Simpson (Valan), page 43.

Printed and Bound in Italy by Lego SpA